AMAZING
BATTLES!

ten by Rosie Peet

Editorial Assistant Rosie Peet
Senior Editor Hannah Dolan
Designer Sandra Perry
Jacket Design David McDonald
Managing Editors Elizabeth Dowsett, Simon Hugo
Pre-Production Producer Marc Staples
Producer Louise Daly
Design Manager Ron Stobbart
Publishing Manager Julie Ferris
Art Director Lisa Lanzarini
Publishing Director Simon Beecroft

Reading Consultant
Linda B. Gambrell, Ph.D

First American Edition, 2016
Published in the United States by DK Publishing
345 Hudson Street, New York, New York 10014

10 9 8 7 6 5 4 3 2 1
007–273729–Jan/15

A WORLD OF IDEAS:
SEE ALL THERE IS TO KNOW

www.dk.com
www.LEGO.com

Contents

Amazing Super Heroes

There are many Super
Heroes in the universe.
Some of the greatest
heroes are Batman,
Wonder Woman, and Superman.

They each have amazing abilities
that help them in their quest
to keep the world safe.
The villains of the world
had better watch out!

Superman

Superman comes from planet Krypton. Now he lives on planet Earth in the city of Metropolis.

Superman hides his superpowers
by having another identity.
His other identity is a newspaper
reporter named Clark Kent.
No one knows that Superman
and Clark Kent are secretly
the same person.

Supergirl is another Super Hero
from planet Krypton.
She sometimes helps
Superman on
his missions.

THE
DAILY

SUPER HEROES

PLANET

SAVE THE DAY

By Lois Lane

The mean, green villain known as Brainiac launched an attack on downtown Metropolis yesterday. Superman and Supergirl defeated the villain and saved our city.

Office worker Fred Jones saw Brainiac invade the city in his gigantic Skull Ship. Mr Jones told the *Daily Planet*, "The Skull Ship was tearing down buildings with its huge tentacles and destroying everything with its scary cannon. It's lucky that Superman and Supergirl were around to save us."

Witnesses saw Superman and Supergirl use their heat vision to destroy the Skull Ship.

This is the latest in a long line of daring rescues by Superman and Supergirl as they continue to keep our city safe.

Brave heroes, Superman and Supergirl

Trouble in Metropolis

Lois Lane is a journalist for the *Daily Planet* newspaper. She writes news stories about Superman. Now she is about to become a news story herself!

General Zod, Faora, and Tor-An are villains from Krypton. They have hatched an evil plot to capture Lois in their Black Zero Dropship.

General Zod

Dangerous Villain

Description: Black hair, bushy eyebrows, angry expression.

Last seen wearing: A black cape and black armor with a silver emblem on his chest.

REWARD: $25,000

Contact us with information about a crime.

MOST WANTED   REPORT A CRIME

Faora

Evil Accomplice to General Zod

Description: Black hair, red lips, scary snarl.

Reward: $10,000

Tor-An

Evil Accomplice to General Zod

Description: Short brown hair, determined grimace.

Reward: $10,000

CLAIM REWARD

Metropolis Rescue

Superman is on a rescue mission! General Zod is holding Lois captive inside his Black Zero Dropship. Can Superman save her?

Superman flies onto the Black Zero Dropship. General Zod puts on his armor and fights Superman. While Superman is battling Zod, Lois runs to the ship's escape pod. She flees to safety, while Superman defeats Zod.

Batman

Batman's mission is to protect Gotham City from crime.
He fights villains with special gadgets and martial arts skills.

Just like Superman, Batman has another identity. Most people know him as the rich businessman Bruce Wayne. At night, Bruce puts on the Batsuit and fights criminals as Batman.

Batman's Gadgets

Bat-Mech
This giant robot gives Batman an advantage over even the strongest foe. Batman controls its movements from the cockpit.

Double Trouble
This arm has two methods of attack. Blasters fire powerful missiles, and a net shooter fires a net to trap enemies.

Batarangs
These weapons whizz through the air so Batman can knock out enemies from a distance.

Robot Hand
The Bat-Mech's left arm has a flexible hand that can grab crooks. Handy!

Breathing Apparatus
When Batman needs to chase enemies underwater, he wears this special tube so he can breathe.

Harpoon Gun
This weapon fires darts that can travel through water at great speed.

The Joker

The Joker is one tricky criminal.
He loves using wacky weapons
to cause mayhem on the
streets of Gotham City.

He is planning to attack the city on a crazy steamroller.

The Joker has lots of henchmen that help him carry out his schemes. He makes them wear clown face paint to match his own face. They are too scared of the Joker to argue!

THE JOKER'S STEAMROLLER

THE JOKER HAS ADDED HIS OWN TWISTS TO THIS MENACING STEAMROLLER.

BOMBS FILLED WITH LAUGHING GAS

GRIN LOOKS LIKE THE JOKER'S INSANE SMILE

CRAZILY COLORFUL ROLLER CAN FLATTEN ENEMIES

WACKY PATTERN ON THE WHEEL

ENOUGH ROOM FOR THE JOKER AND ONE CLOWN-LIKE HENCHMAN

Battle for Gotham City

Whoosh! Here comes Batman
in his speedy Batwing.
He is rushing to defend
Gotham City from the Joker.

The Joker is attacking the city on his scary steamroller. It is flattening everything in its path! The Joker fires laughing-gas bombs, but the Batwing dodges them. Batman swoops down to stop the steamroller in its tracks.

Wonder Woman

Wonder Woman has some special tools that help her defeat villains. When villains are caught in her Lasso of Truth, they confess their crimes.

Wonder Woman also has an Invisible Jet. Her Invisible Jet can't be seen by her enemies, so she can use it to sneak up on them.

Heroes Unite

There is a terrifying new
threat to the world's safety.
A very strong and clever
crook is planning a fiendish
raid on Gotham City.

These Super Heroes will need to work together as a team in order to put a stop to this villain's monkey business...

31

Gorilla Grodd

Gorilla Grodd is an evil gorilla. He is very intelligent, and is always thinking about his next wicked plot. He has even invented a special mind-control device that he wears on his head.

His latest plan is to attack Gotham City and steal the city's bananas. Gorilla Grodd loves bananas and will stop at nothing to get his hairy hands on them.

33

INSIDE THE MIND
OF GORILLA
GRODD

What thoughts cross the mind of an evil gorilla?

Tomorrow I will raid Gotham City for bananas.

I will rise at dawn to get a head start. The early gorilla gets the banana, hahaha!

Banana Battle

Gorilla Grodd is feeling hungry!
He spots a banana delivery truck
and decides to steal bananas
from it. Greedy Grodd lifts the
truck into the air and shakes it,
sending the bananas flying.
The poor driver
is terrified!

Here comes Batman in his Bat-Mech! He stomps toward Grodd. Uh-oh! Watch out for that banana, Batman! The Bat-Mech slips and falls with a crash. Batman needs backup!

DRIVER'S DAILY LOG

All delivery activities must be logged daily by all drivers.

DATE:	TIME:	NOTES:
Yesterday	9.00am	Picked up bananas
	10.00am	Delivered bananas
	11.00am	Picked up bananas
	Midday	Delivered bananas

DATE:	TIME:	NOTES:
Today	9.00am	Picked up bananas
	10.00am	Delivered bananas
	11.00am	Picked up bananas
	Midday	Attacked by an evil gorilla!

Super Heroes' Victory

Wonder Woman swoops in on her
Invisible Jet. Gorilla Grodd can't
see her! She takes aim and fires
the jet's missiles at Grodd,
taking him by surprise.

Next, Superman arrives and uses
his super-strength to deliver a
knockout blow to Gorilla Grodd.
Grodd is finally defeated!
The Super Heroes worked
as a team to save the day.
Good job, Super Heroes!

Quiz

1. Where does Superman live?

2. Which Super Hero uses special gadgets?

3. Which villain has a steamroller?

4. What does Gorilla Grodd like to eat?

5. What does Wonder Woman use to sneak past her enemies?

6. Where does General Zod hold Lois Lane captive?

7. Which Super Hero has a Lasso of Truth?

8. What is the name of Batman's other identity?

Answers on page 45.

Glossary

captive
unable to escape

confess
to tell the truth, or
own up to something

fiendish
wicked and mean

gadgets
useful devices

invisible
can't be seen

intelligence
valuable information

journalist
someone who
writes for a
newspaper

martial arts
sports that teach
fighting skills
or self-defense

mayhem
a crazy, out of
control situation

unite
join together

victory
a big win

Index

Answers to the quiz on pages 42 and 43:
1. Metropolis 2. Batman 3. The Joker 4. Bananas 5. Her Invisible Jet
6. The Black Zero Dropship 7. Wonder Woman 8. Bruce Wayne

Guide for Parents

This book is part of an exciting four-level reading series for children, developing the habit of reading widely for both pleasure and information. These chapter books have a compelling main narrative to suit your child's reading ability. Each book is designed to develop your child's reading skills, fluency, grammar awareness, and comprehension in order to build confidence and engagement when reading.

Ready for a *Level 2* book

YOUR CHILD SHOULD

- be familiar with using beginning letter sounds and context clues to figure out unfamiliar words.
- be aware of the need for a slight pause at commas and a longer one at periods.
- alter his/her expression for questions and exclamations.

A VALUABLE AND SHARED READING EXPERIENCE

For many children, reading requires much effort, but adult participation can make this both fun and easier. So here are a few tips on how to use this book with your child.

TIP 1 Check out the contents together before your child begins:
- read the text about the book on the back cover.
- flip through the book and stop to chat about the contents page together to heighten your child's interest and expectation.
- make use of unfamiliar or difficult words on the page in a brief discussion.
- chat about the nonfiction reading features used in the book, such as headings, captions, lists, or charts.